PICTURES OF
3 SEASONS
GAIL RIXEN

graphics by Ross Zirkle

Minnesota Voices Project Number 47

NEW RIVERS PRESS 1991

Edited by Susan Welch
Cover and inside artwork by Ross Zirkle
Book Design by Gaylord Schanilec
Typesetting by Peregrine Publications

The author wishes to extend special thanks to the following people for their in-
fluences over the years: Tim Kroeger, Gloria Rixen, Mary Thorndycraft, Martin Carter,
Betty Rixen, and Morris Rixen.

Some of the poems in this collection have appeared in the following publications:
*Loonfeather, Mankato Poetry Review, Menomonie Review, The Northland Review,
Plainswoman, Poets of Southwestern Minnesota, Studio One, Sundog, Visions, Whittier
Globe,* and *Writer's Premiere.* Our thanks to the editors for allowing us to reprint these
poems here.

The publication of *Pictures of Three Seasons* has been made possible by grant sup-
port from the Jerome Foundation, the Arts Development Fund of the United Arts
Council, the Beverly J. and John A. Rollwagen Fund of the Minneapolis Foundation,
Cray Research Foundation, the Elizabeth A. Hale Fund of the Minneapolis Founda-
tion, the First Bank System Foundation, Liberty State Bank, the Star Tribune/Cowles
Media Company, the Tennant Company Foundation, the Valspar Corporation, and
the National Endowment for the Arts (with funds appropriated by the Congress of
the United States). New Rivers also wishes to thank the Minnesota Non-Profits
Assistance Fund for its invaluable support.

New Rivers Press books are distributed by

The Talman Company
150-5th Avenue
New York, NY 10011

Bookslinger
2402 University Avenue, Suite 507
Minneapolis, MN 55114

Pictures of Three Seasons has been manufactured in the United States of America
for New Rivers Press (C. W. Truesdale, Editor/Publisher), 420 N. 5th Street/Suite
910, Minneapolis, MN 55401, in a first edition of 1,200 copies.

*Dedicated to
the memory of
Roxanne E. Wilson,
1954–1976*

CONTENTS

I. All This Dancing

3 It Starts Somewhere
4 Pictures of Three Seasons
5 August
6 Going Back to the Bar
7 Testing Distances
8 April
9 R.
10 Crossing the River
11 Keys
12 Prairie July
13 Three Day Blizzard
14 Some Weather Turns
15 A Modern Judgment
16 Sucker Spearing
17 Cold Snap
18 "No one talks about this" – Rakosi
19 Hot Night
20 Young Pigs on Adventure
21 Incantation Against Suicide
22 Of All the Dust
23 In a Dim Nest
24 Custom Denied
25 Learning to See Again
26 Dream
27 After a Winter Warm Spell
28 The One that Fought Back

II. Scenes from a Passerby

33 So You Want to Know about Coon Hunting
34 After the Bars Close
35 His Mother
36 The Junkman
37 After Her Divorce
38 Finnish Women in the Summer Kitchen
39 Fossum
40 The Bond
41 In the Pasture Near Locherbie
42 The Town Fool
43 Instructions for Secession
44 Corline Man
45 Prodigal at the Deathbed
46 Right about Now
47 Melvin Quits Farming
48 The Reading
49 Spring; Letting the Cows Out
50 Ida Marie
51 Loner
52 Buck Fever
54 Fall Plowing
55 The Last Child Goes
56 English Teacher
57 Alice's Romance
58 The Warranty
59 Hunter in Winter
60 Old Men Who Stand on the Streetcorners
61 Father of Many
62 The Man in 103
63 Sudden Calm

ALL THIS
DANCING

IT STARTS SOMEWHERE

Back when margarine was oleo and white,
residents of Broken Nose with reason to go
crossed Iowa's wide borders
by camper and station wagon.
In clandestine runs by dead of night,
packages wrapped in coolers next to bologna,
and boxes hidden in spare-tire wells,
came home to foil the butter boys.

A secret roared in beery fishhouses
and whispered about over the fences,
the only little sin set out for company
started a snowball rolling.

In no time, dogs roamed alleys.
Working men found a Jim's Cafe dinner
no longer too big to finish.
Ernst started opening on Sundays.
Children spent good money
on pinball and foosball.

It's been sin ever since,
beer cans in the ditch,
and yellow oleo
sold right out front in the case.

PICTURES OF THREE SEASONS

The camera eye is never my eye —
too distant, too late.

I wanted to show you
pheasants and bluejays fighting in the dead garden.
I had a sequence of sunsets, looking southwest,
five days of brilliance defying dull drifts.
And there were pictures of me,
hair done up, laughing —
you wouldn't know me.

All this I tried to save in your absence
through long days working in dim attics
and in the heat of a drought summer.
Somehow the pictures do not show what I saw.
Something about the lack of light
or slow film or the distance.

You see here shapes hung in gray air,
light and shadow
and faces caught on bad sides,
just two dimensions requiring explanations.

You really should have been there.
I swear there was more.

AUGUST

August.
In the stillness,
mist hangs above corn tassels.
Early afternoon is lit with gulls
turning white, gray sides
as they whirl
like leaves caught in a dust devil.
A quarter section's newly dug
but they do not light there.

I eat supper,
something left over.
Then, in air sweet with overripe crabapples,
wings beat close above.
Gulls circle, swoop, rise above the yard,
so close they all have different faces.
Expressionless, they pass without a glance,
yet they know I am there,
just not important.

GOING BACK TO THE BAR

Gray men and old lovers lean like gargoyles
over the precipice of the bar,
boozy and intent on something from that height,
who reared back laughing back then
in smoky cars passing something around,
and later the two of us
stirring and stirring
the tonic that cured for days.

Turning, one of the leaners catches my arm,
looks long, then mumbles,
"I thought you were someone else."
The hand cannot hold and drops away.

The band is loud.
Baseless, I wander and sit,
wander and sit.
The moon's a beer clock
that slowly turns and cannot set,
languid with inert drive,
a pinioned sphere that takes no captives.

TESTING DISTANCES

Testing distances,
owls murmur between groves.
The moon's caught in elm branches
and hangs helplessly silent.
Dog shadows on the lawn
wait and watch.

I have not seen you for months.
There's prairie between
and no common tongue.

Someone's dog warns Keep Away
to stars, lovers, enemies,
and the owls are telling the old joke again.
The one in which we are the punch line.

APRIL

Such wildness in the air!
The river is running fast and wide,
taking the swamps when it will.

A wind is blowing something up,
sucking curtains out the window
and chasing dust in a spin
across a gray field.
Dry corn leaves clatter as they circle
and rise faster and faster,
then drop straight down,
still, on the cracked ground.

Tentative quackgrass greens along the plowing,
so slowly,
taking days to show itself
as the river races,
rampant and impatient of one
who waits on the bank,
sluggish and wrapped so tightly in human skin,
in its winter of being.

R.

Our promises to remember in old age
included a seventy-year-old you
in your plane buzzing my cabin.
I would wave my old arms so.
But your green bones in their grave
never meant to wait.

Already I'm waving wildly,
perhaps to chase you off
as you buzz me,
kamakazi you.
Perhaps I await the crash
and am waving you back.
A sky this heavy with longing
will not support you long.

What a hard promise you keep.
How roughly you bound the bargain.

CROSSING THE RIVER

Withered cranberries hang
among bromegrass and willow.
Popples on the river's south side
have tumbled in.
I always meant to make a bridge there,
since the crossing was deep.

We take the ice route,
far enough from the beaver dam
to hold us.
Single file, spaced out.

It has been an easy winter
and he wants to drag the beavers' leavings
home for firewood before heavy snows.
So much down wood here.

We gather fungi from dead trees for decorations
and have careful little to say.
I meant to be here.
I meant to go.

KEYS

could always tell he was coming
by the clinking of keys
    crucifixes

told him once
we didn't need his goddamn keys
but he laughed
Try To Get In Those Doors Without Them

left him smirking
and picked every lock
smashed every door

when he came he beat us good
but hugged us and whimpered
My Poor Naughty Children

We stole his keys, too.

PRAIRIE JULY

Sometimes it is so quiet
I lie awake all night
hearing clouds creak by.

Swallows swarm on the wires at dusk.
Fireflies roar by the screen at night.
Just for the sweetness of it
pelicans rise from Frog Lake
and soar high in great floating circles
above the farm.
Their white bodies nearly disappear
against the sky,
then slowly drop to still waters,
taking the afternoon with them.

For weeks now the big round bales
have waited in a row for a place,
for some reason
to roll.

THREE DAY BLIZZARD

Throughout the night, wind tore the shed roof off
and slapped the pieces against the house.
The house creaked with each blast.
Wind found every crack, filled it with dirt.
Nothing's sacred.
Even the penitent come in dirty-faced, beaten.

Did I tell you I hate this country?
I dream of beaches in California,
getting down to one layer of clothing.
I want to throw off Scandinavian distance
and talk to strangers.

In the morning, both doors are drifted tight.
I crawl out a window
and follow a drift over the house.
The barn is lost,
on its way to some grove in Iowa.

I promise to leave this country
but the wind wants more.
It must have me crawl to the woodshed
and fight for breath coming back with loads.
My dog is lost and the chickens are hungry.
I am beyond yelling, past struggle.

If you want me to die,
then take me, wind.
I give up.
If I survive this,
I will join a Lutheran church.

SOME WEATHER TURNS

The wide harvested fields,
the barren alkaline lands of Saskatchewan
bring back our times.
Some slow methodical derrick
knows our tempo.
It was the beat of the cool flesh,
the shrug-shouldered intimacies
that pretended our freedom.

Sometimes my heart was as big as the prairie sky;
it would have taken you in.
Can you tell me why September warms by day
what it freezes by night,
shrugging every land toward winter?

A MODERN JUDGMENT:
ON SEEING BRUEGEL'S *The Triumph of Death*

They sit around the kitchen table
watching you slim and sick on T.V.,
noting plagues and prophesies,
how this new virus falls into His scheme of things.
Someone quotes Revelations.
God's will you die.
His judgment's against you for what you call love.

It is no longer a virus.
They look for corrupt vapors,
the buboes of sin,
a weak wrist or tracks,
our new Stars of David.
Their God purges.
The wages of sin is death.

In Bruegel's scene,
skeletons slay in the shadow of the cross,
the supper table's strewn,
a child screams in sick arms,
a man sings love, love to a maiden
as a boney arm slides around her waist
and no voice cries Amen.

SUCKER SPEARING

The river is deep, spread into swamps,
still between hummocks.
We pole and float the jon boat
through clear, fast waters.
We wait, spears just under the surface.

They come in groups, determined,
heading through the deeps
till they come under us.
We do not breathe or move.

We lunge and they shoot away, unhurt.
Water magnifies, distorts, puts off our aim.
We try the shore, blame the sun,
shuffle home with none.

That was eighteen years ago.
In dreams, I stab now murky waters,
wanting clear vision, sure aim.
I throw and throw.
I look up to you and you are balding,
sitting darkly at the back of the boat.
I ask, "What am I doing wrong?"

Our white beach is grown over.
The water's greenish.
You do not answer.

COLD SNAP

Cold snap in August.
The house sets its rough haunches into dry dirt,
warns squash finally blooming
not to get big ideas.

Again I have sat too long in summer shade.
It will not be summer again,
even if hot mists hang in the cornfields.
Nights will all be cool,
quilt nights,
nights when dreams remember far back
and awaken sleepers with a shiver.

As though a familiar body turned to go,
there's vacancy in drying grasses,
memory of silence, loss.
I am immutably turned toward hermitage,
the prison of the awkward and unforgiven.
I know what I can survive,
but I mourn the face turning away in autumn,
leaving me a thin coat
and no goodbye.

No one talks about this
                    – Rakosi

Long past the killing blow and the low moan,
cooks prepare steaks with gloved hands.
We do not talk of it over dinner,
when talk is polite, civilized.
We rename this flesh and bone meat,
twirl on silvered forks
what was leg, life.

Only savage men hunt and kill,
hanging the dead like medals.
Cruel farmers watch terrified eyes go dull,
the blood pulse streaming to the ground.

We are not such people.
Man has risen from rough ways.
We applaud the clarity of broth.

HOT NIGHT

Bear in its cave,
heat dens in the upstairs bedroom
where no wind dares rout it.
Neighbor dogs warn back and forth only twice;
claims rest unsettled by mutual consent.

In the stagnant room,
captive of the dull beast
that tosses me for its pleasure,
one loud mosquito wanders the darkness;
I bare myself in ambush.

Sometime in the darkness
a breeze gathers its voyeur courage,
creeping in through the screen,
only to leaf through a *National Geographic*.

YOUNG PIGS ON ADVENTURE

They lined up at the gate for days
watching for a change of scene.

One of them, then all, found the fence flaw.
They followed the barn through tall weeds
to the front where the dog lay in the shade.
They surrounded him,
twenty, thirty ditto copies,
smelling his fur, looking him over.

The dog awoke with a start –
some canine nightmare come real –
ten paces they followed him away.
He turned on them and chased,
scattering retreating pigs
back into the barn in a whirl of dust.
He lay again.

They lined up and peered out between the boards.
All afternoon they harassed the dog,
sneaking out for tag, racing for home,
till evening hung its still veil over the place.

In the dark barn
one grunted now and then
about the garden, just up,
unfenced.

INCANTATION AGAINST SUICIDE

She dreamt, she said, of a tight passage
between two cliffs
where a man more beautiful than life
waited in a flowing white feather cape
on a very green spot.
She was squeezing through to him
when she awoke,
and two weeks later died at her own hand.

She spoke his spell.
You make magic against him.
Find if he is flesh or image.
Call through the crack
for what kindness he can offer.
Pass the place for weeks
to see if he will come to you.

If he does not,
seal up the passage with spit and anger.
Chink it with a thousand curses that say I AM.

But if he comes,
holding out his pure, grim hand,
hear me calling curses for you,
shouting your virtues like stones against him,
and stay,
stay!

OF ALL THE DUST

Of all the dust
that for haphazard eons assembled stars,
burned blue-hot,
or wandered the frigid darkness,
from all that innocent dust we came,
beings with thought and conscience,
building our own destruction.
Our bombs fell reckless of the peacemakers.

Our last few fled to the icy caps,
dreaming of green prairies,
of leaves ticking together in breezes.
Never again will sweet clover bloom for them
or memories include the living.

Now whales singing at sea
gossip about a little land animal
that raged against the earth
with a fury that left nothing safe.

And in the rubble the dust lies,
never again to assemble a being
that could dream of the stars
and plan wars.

IN A DIM NEST

In a dim nest of poets
beer pop and cigarettes are lit
and the poems begin.
Arms orchestrate.
There is great humor here,
a tag game of wit,
where if you laugh, you're out.
Absurdity and irony drag the sun
below the windowsill
where the thugs dissect it.

Then he reads.
The room begins to fill
with the scents of his scenes.
A hero's lost,
drug as a corpse before us.
A wasted life hangs as a piñata
to be struck at by laughing children.
Gods wallow in ashes.

In a place still busy and exotic,
jesters begin again
hauling in grandiose gray.

CUSTOM DENIED

They needed something from the attic
and boosted me into the darkness.
I didn't want to go
where I stumbled blindly
on hands and knees through old dust,
afraid of what hands could find next.

The gray-haired ladies at the hole
called up directions,
reaching their ringed fingers
for something left
among potty chairs and old diaries.
Past The Canner, they called.
By The Cradle.
Past His Want And Your Nothing.
There Where God Placed You, they said.
Give It Up.

I awoke in a sweat and shook,
trying to detail to him
what I would not hand down.

LEARNING TO SEE AGAIN
– after a decision to quit writing

What's the worth of all this dancing, anyway?
So much circling around the real.
A hermit with too much free time
interprets nature and bemoans fate.

Look out over the landscape
and see only sky, tree, snow, grass –
no message in the evergreen, just wind.
Let well enough alone.
No matter that the air is eerie
with goose wails
as V after V aims north,
that your hunting dog runs in circles,
leaping, searching,
never thinking of looking up.

DREAM

You are out on Shipman Lake.
Sunshine. No wind.
The metal boat is cold,
the dark water stirred by deep springs.
You pull up sunfish, bluegill, and bullheads.
The man says the lake cannot be swum;
the cold currents cramp swimmers.

Then you are riding a boat
tied to shore, twelve feet out,
over water dropped off to blackness.
The sandy access rises sparkling before you.
You will not turn around in the seat
to the vertigo of this suspension.
Weightless legs could never touch bottom
and weeds would tangle and drag you under
to whatever waits there.
Sit at dead center and do not rock.
You are ten years old and cannot swim.
You distrust the substance
of what you cannot see.

Spruce and popple stand back on high ground,
making no move to help.
They know how the dead lie
and will not say.

AFTER A WINTER WARM SPELL

Determined,
chasing scared clouds southeast,
cold comes back to the prairie.
No birds in the gray grove,
just high winds that monotonously play elms
for foreboding moans.
Old snow lies fixed with dog tracks
and stuck with young trees,
skeletons without a murmur.
I gather wood against chastening predictions.

Only man takes portents from weather,
must expect storms after warming,
but naive deer move freely today
and pheasants settle in with full crops
where they will.
Cattle lie on bare spots
and chew their cuds,
looking out over the west yard
that will be green and white
and green again,
only that.

THE ONE THAT FOUGHT BACK

Inevitably
the cat feigns disinterest,
then strikes again.
Testing mouse mettle,
it drags the gray mass back
to the smothering smell of cat
where, cradled in paws,
its heartbeat shakes the ground.

The cat grows bored, wants action,
sits back and bats the beast
that rises on its hind legs
fiercely to defend or attack,
that leaps on the cat's nose,
rides the shake, squeals,
and must be bitten down,
laid out broken,
fur and meat.

SCENES FROM
A PASSERBY

SO YOU WANT TO KNOW ABOUT COON HUNTING

That takes me back years,
when the sound of the hounds would wake me
in the middle of the night,
not sad like coyotes or loons,
but the sound of death coming
on the fury of sixteen legs
with the mercy of canine teeth
and all so sudden that you remember
how the cold night breezes in that woods
chill you to the bone,
how every tree seems to have
a pair of eyes staring down.
Makes you wonder who's being chased,
alien to the dark woods.

Kid, it wasn't the hunting I feared
but the coming back
to that bed that night
alive.

AFTER THE BARS CLOSE

Maybe his fried eggs know
who he is talking suicide to.
Smarter than the college fools,
stoned and sprawling over the counter,
he would rather be dead.

He counts jail cells on two hands
and hospitals on one;
something always contains him.
Now cigarette smoke threatens to erase him.
If he knew it, he'd swing.
But he's talking to someone.
It could be me.

Behind him,
only a pane of glass away,
rain on the tar is trapped by streetlights;
a thousand diamonds are set free to
sparkle.

HIS MOTHER

She still refuses to go,
lives on muffins and jelly
and that confused marmalade of hers.
She forgets him in mid-sentence
and leaves for something sweet
put up years before
without leaving her chair.

He asks doctors how she survives
with all the wrong ingredients
to his recipe.
When he comes with firm intent
and a moving truck,
she isn't fooled
and tells her rocker
"I won't be back."

THE JUNKMAN

Grease and rust are the humors of this world.
Motion and decomposition call this graveyard home
and course within this fenced body
with eternal determination.

These preparations I sell are no healers;
they are all we can ask of iron.
My flesh always wanted more –
cures with no traces of the hurts.
Sharp beginnings and endings are never so sure
as the wait
till time comes to lay
its worn workings down with me.

AFTER HER DIVORCE

This was life with him:
the dark storm looks
of men who gather to exile women
and the young hostilities churning to rage.
I got to be crazy for roofs against cloudbursts,
always afraid to offend.
My hands got the nagging itch
to fix anything broken,
to fill the world with coarse, functional things.

What kind of question
is "What's for supper?"
I needed a test of goodness, not will.
Daily affection dwindled to courtesy.
I drew a line he could not see or cross,
lay in the cool nights a stranger to him.
I told him, even then,
I would give up my life for him,
knowing it would never come to that.

I still tell people that,
for the heroics of the thought,
just to picture him so impotent,
so beaten,
so injured a mass brooding in his silence.

FINNISH WOMEN IN THE SUMMER KITCHEN

They serve the fire.
Indifferently, it rolls steam
off the canner
by them through the screen.

But for the digital watches,
they could be their mothers.
Finnish or English,
the rhythm's the same,
rolls off like a hard boil.
They talk about the season,
measuring out spices with their hands.
Some gossip about a neighbor's microwave.
Someone's kid gone bad
or hanging out-of-season deer.

What they do not say
drips into the jars to wait
till cold January to whisper
in the quiet house.

It's all gone now but the name,
sold out.
They came in on wooden wheels
and drove away on radials.
I just moved across the street
and sat down.

The new highway took business to bigger towns,
left us sitting like dolls on the empty streets –
dolls, who once fixed working parts
and put things in motion.

Sometimes when light comes in the shop window
and lands right there,
I can see Mabel in her rosy apron
and the stances of old friends.
Then I can smell the heat in the coals,
feel the weight of the hammer,
and the metal that made our workings turn.

These days my new birdhouses swing in the trees,
pretty and empty, no good to anything.
Iron's dependable, keeps to its bounds.
Circumstance roughly pounds
the shape of my days.

THE BOND

When fathers run their little worlds hard,
as they were run,
and mothers do not have will,
and daughters are raised for export,
they do not come back.

Louise went seven hundred miles
for a job, not a husband,
just went, and did not come back
until the funeral.

She waited in the house grown smaller in adult memory,
heard her mother's tentative heels again on the wooden floor,
recognized the faces stirring uneasily in the small kitchen.
Dishes not quite clean now,
walls in need of paint.

He lay in his padded box
shrunken and white,
remote as voice is to stone,
jaw still set.

She had thought they would let her go now,
the stooped woman and her sovereign, saying
Go, Do As You Will In This Happy Life.

But both kept their sullen silence
every day when she came to the mound,
her restless hands working the wanton fallen twigs,
breaking them always in halves, fourths, eighths.

IN THE PASTURE NEAR LOCHERBIE

Seven generations of my family walked this grass,
children herding cattle,
old men leaning on walking sticks,
boys chasing sparrows with slingshots –
but never before this grim hunt.

As a child,
I lost a jackknife somewhere in these pastures –
my first jackknife.
I retraced my tracks for weeks,
eyes to the ground,
seeing a glint in the grass
or shapes that could be,
but never were,
my knife.

I remember it today,
hoping for a glance of it
and not something human.
Smoke from the smoldering houses
follows us as we search,
shoulder to shoulder,
strangers, townsfolk, and kin,
over land that will never be mine again,
that keeps its treasures of flesh and blood
and gives up only bits of cloth and metal.

THE TOWN FOOL

Driving home from town,
his face was still red.
For days he heard their smooth impatient words
remembering his mistakes.
Eldon in the wrong line,
tongue-tied again.
The cows just kept chewing dully
as he renamed them
for bankers and cashiers.

Towards evening
he watched his cat
walking unconcerned as swallows divebombed,
each graceful swoop a near hit.

Dreaming there on the step,
he saw her turn each time,
pulling a sleek flying thing
out of the sky.

INSTRUCTIONS FOR SECESSION

Say you hate me.
Now you'll have no history
as you wished,
no kin to draw the hard lines
of your memory,
no familiar voice
to surprise you with disagreement.
Keeping tradition,
we begin a long, silent feud.

Say you do not see,
when you pass a mirror,
the shape of my jaw,
a glance of my eyes.
I will not mention aloud
the folly of family pictures,
your captured smile
I cannot help but return
when I leaf aimlessly
through photograph albums.

Save your pride
if I forget myself,
calling with some foolish news
to hear the sound of the voice
that harmonized like no one else.
Save yourself and hang up.

CORLINE MAN

We were strangers in the country church.
He and his family had a side corner;
he, the aisle seat.
Atop an old black suit,
his purple wad of face
hung nearly to his chest.
He must have had eyes.

I stared, through "a poor miserable sinner,"
as the pastor promised us death, shame, and misery,
and as parishioners sang with such fervor
"Free from Satan's Tyranny,"
rising in the vengeful oak benches with new authority.

Parents turned our heads,
directed us toward the words
that blew so harmlessly past their unruffled ears.
It was what to do on Sunday,
the standing together, the singing,
clean clothes,
the reprimands to recite,
the defects to find.

But through all the ceremony
I could not take my eyes off the purple man –
the folds of his face were so familiar,
his sin so defiantly worn.

Sitting in a beige room,
the air still yet crackling,
bitterness washes away.
Anger, the haughty old hermit,
dies in another room without human touch.
Leave him to it.

Take up the hand that never touched,
never in leaving,
never with love.
Recount the years —
all forgiven —
no need to say.
The stranger in the bed
at last is old,
at last has three names, not one,
a whole history loosely bound with yours.

But ties cannot hold.
They fall from the bed so easily
and tangle you up,
drag you numbly home.
Alone now,
king in a child's house,
crow and crow your triumphant sobs.

RIGHT ABOUT NOW

Right about now she'd be back from the mailbox
sitting in her dim kitchen
deciding about him
after thinking real late in bed last night
with that starving moon
barely making an outline of the window.

She would go out after lunch
after the dew and morning chill
to the garden grown smaller every year
to check the growth never growth enough.
Still the same tune if she sings.

He knew just how the woods would seem
this time of year,
lonesome and cool,
and how her voice could say,
"Don't you come here anymore."

MELVIN QUITS FARMING

Frost, that creeping boil of earth,
brings them up every year
to foil him.
Peppered anew,
the fields lie brown and lifeless now.

At seventy-five,
he will not pick rock this year,
done with all that turmoil.
Leave it to a younger man,
who'd stand pleased with his stoneboat load,
thinking he's done.

The reaper sinks on the bullwheel.
The corn picker's a birdhouse.
If the river meanders wild,
let it take the planted evergreens.
This stir does not grow old:
wind, water, earth.

THE READING

As she read
she stirred the angry pot,
boiling memory
to a bitter concentrate.

Meat of sacrifice,
salt of silence,
turnip turned strong from drought,
magic that made children,
suppers, home
swirled in a pot with one handle,
her hand burning
holding it over the flame.

Years in a kitchen
brewed this day.
Take a taste,
husband,
children,
listener.

SPRING; Letting the Cows Out

The youngstock,
and they are all young today,
burst from the door,
kicking concrete-crippled legs high
in a winter's stretch.
One is stuck to the belly
in the manure pile, bellering.
The old holstein's bag swings so wide
as she trots,
it nearly topples her.

The dog scoots under the gate,
determined to order this outrage.
Heads down, cows vanquish him
yelping away.

People watch from the board fence
no small foot dares climb.
All this foolishness and
a poor milking tonight.
Already the oldest child kicks dirt in disgust;
dirt that confounds,
that dries out dead,
will be his without joy or question.

Forgetting himself,
the youngest child hops up and down soundlessly
as the last cow out
comes to life again.

IDA MARIE

Ida Marie cut her long hair off
when she was thirty-five.
It fell soft and shining in the pail,
the color of young men's backs
glistening in their fieldwork.

So far from town and neighbors,
too far for a Sunday drive,
even if a man had reason.
Ida comforted herself knowing
that prairie roses bloomed, seen or not.
The same God that sent hail sent rain.

She could quote Scripture on patience.
She could busy herself all winter long
and dream dreams that would put
a prairie sunset to shame,
but the only visions that ever took their place
were sweet william blooms around the house
and even they turned brown
for the lack and the want.

LONER

After three days alone,
she thinks she is only eyes, watching,
and stops laughing at TV comedies.
If the phone rings,
the sound of her voice shocks her;
it knows what to say.

She begins to like the smell of her skin.
Time loses its marks.
Light comes and goes without fanfare.
Nothing is imperative.

Moonlight calls her sometimes
into the blue fields
and wide prairie silences.

When she dreams,
she is showing a picture of herself to
people.
When she asks if they know this woman,
they shake their heads soberly.

BUCK FEVER

The woods are still.
The stand rocks beneath him
and silence seems a loud static.
Somewhere a squirrel rustles leaves.
There! A tree groans against another.
He is waiting for the deer.

By noon the wind picks up
and he eats an apple,
throwing the core into the brush.
Thoughts move through his mind
like the scent of apple on the wind.
He dreams of the future.
A strange self rises up,
busy and big,
but less constant than one twig
in this old woods.

Then, a sound.
Down the riverbottom the brush cracks.
He is coming.
The stand is reeling now.
He rides it like a sparrow rides a blowing bough,
every cell listening.
A blade of grass is moved aside –
the dirt cries out.
The buck snorts.

After a long rigid time he walks again.
His head comes into view,
then his shoulder.
The human blood burns in the veins;
his eyes barely see.
The sides move in and out
in a perfect hide that is almost the man's own,
magnificent and haughtily racked.

At last he breathes,
a low longing moan of air,
animal as the buck's breath.
The metal hangs foreign still
and long past the white tail's goodbye
he does not know himself.

FALL PLOWING

In the cab the radio tells him
Snow tonight.

The dark clouds of winter
crowd around the leafless northwest grove
impatiently.

Behind him the wounded earth rolls over
and awaits its windy diminishing.
White gulls swoop and light behind the plow,
extending grace to him
one more season.

Go.
Sentimentality's the fool face
I too often wear.
Just go.

I am always in a doorway
waving goodbye,
always constant,
a survivor.
I am freed by absences,
leveled by loss.
I live well with only export.

Wind wears me;
age saps.
I am less for waving.
Take the road.
I have much to do.

ENGLISH TEACHER
for D.M.

The Great American Novel waits in his head,
the spelling corrected, the structure reworked.
Every day he sings others' words,
the images that lift the heart.
He tells the truth of ages,
translates voices that shyly whisper.

They shift uneasily in hard seats,
would begrudge him dirges.
Hamlet's a poor second
to the next six pack.
Iambic pentameter's condensed to four letters.

Hear the melody of the words,
he pleads; he harasses.
He pretends not to see
the kid in the back row
quickly cover his own scribbled epic
as he walks by.
He imagines his song taken up, harmonized.

"Once."
She stopped wringing her tissue.
Winter outside the picture window
held its breath.

"He got up from cards one night
and stood behind me –
not a word –
but took the pins from my hair
one by one without pulling
and smoothed it down my back
and combed it with his fingers –
and him a hired man!

"I sat there unable to move
as goosebumps raced over me
but he did nothing.
He owned me then
but he took no license,
just filled the cookstove
and went to bed."

She turned her red face to the window.

"I had a good husband and seven children
but never anything to move me like that,
never."

THE WARRANTY

Blame and guilt have always been her servants.
On their words, men did her bidding
and children slunk along the right path.
No one will listen here.
They want eating and defecating
and cannot be shamed.
She has sent herself to bed without supper
and now lies dying.
Someone will pay for a poor prognosis.
She points a whitened finger
as though you backed the warranty.

HUNTER IN WINTER

Whittled from memory,
popple and catalpa ducks float
on the kitchen table slough.

It is the off season,
but he is still there,
humped on the muddy edge
where cattails and rushes
whisper their dry conversations.

They are returning from feeding.
Come Down, he calls,
Come Down To Your Kin.
They are leery and call back to him,
circling once, twice.
Finally they set their wings.

Flushed with waiting,
he raises his knife
and with stroke after stroke,
gives them back to the sky.

OLD MEN WHO STAND ON THE STREETCORNERS

When beef and hog trucks roll through
the sultry box that is main street,
he squeals and bawls along
against a larger cage
that keeps him poor and pitiful.

In this city of long stares out of windows
and Harvard accents in corn country,
faces wear industry:
each crease is a road to wealth,
each glance a judgment of worth.
Their eyes chase him
bellering up the chute,
canner and cutter,
the unprime.

He drove all the way home in second,
this master of his salvage paradise.
Father of many,
killer of bears,
a thousand legends spring
from the little man's face.

Some remember the gun, loaded, frozen
under the eave all winter,
the fifty-odd cars on the hill,
his roaming herds of horses.

Those who knew his father
wait for the day when he goes,
just goes,
way up north into the trees,
leaving a wife to wonder what he was.

THE MAN IN 103

A studied indulgence, madness?
A timely vacation from sense?
No. The sky was too blue
or the silence too quiet
or some voice said more than it said.
No matter.
Nothing's benign about white ceilings.
The legs of chairs are so sad.

It wasn't always so.
Once this child spoke
and eyes did not stare back queerly.
"I see," they say now
and let me be.
Once I followed after, explaining.
Then days of humdrum.
Hours that required action
went of their own volition.

Nothing new in the yard.
Awkward hollyhocks climb high
and scream color unheard.
But, then, what's done is done.

No coming rain,
no reason for silence.
The sudden quiet startles me.

A measure's taken,
an extract made:
Who are you that hangs on the wall
in black and white,
enduring in name only on the mailbox?
Who had I seen in the child's picture
drawn in the clear, slow dreaming
of the wait,
the one
perfect in moments,
in postures?
Over thirteen years
you have penciled yourself in.
An empty chair and a roomful of things,
headlights that sometimes turn in,
always in danger of fading.

In the hard truth of the sudden calm,
I wield the eraser.

Wind comes up again
like nothing's changed.

was born in 1954 and raised on a farm near Park Rapids, Minnesota. Since graduation from the University of Minnesota-Morris, she has worked as a self-employed carpenter (10 years), a substitute teacher, and co-editor of the small magazine, *Sundog*. Her work has appeared in many small magazines and her collaborations with Park Rapids visual artist Ross Zirkle have appeared in many libraries.

"Creative writing captured me in high school, where I had very tolerant and supportive teachers. Writing has always been something I *had* to do, not only as a log of personal history, but as a way of speaking to and about the world around me. Poetry, I've found, evokes and crystallizes thought in a way no other communication can." Rixen has written poetry for 20 years.